"It is clear from *Advance You, ...age* mat Lori is divinely inspired and on a mission to propel people forward with poise and self-confidence and to bring the beauty within each person out in the best possible light. As a career advisor to college students turned image consultant to musicians and others, Lori has an excellent take on the big picture for how personal image plays into career development planning."
Stevie Puckett, Career Tips blog

"Great for anyone who wants to make a good first impression and improve their personal brand. I gained valuable insight into improving my appearance and becoming more aware of how I present myself."
Mike Coleman, business strategist and author

"During my presidency at O'More College of Design, Lori Bumgarner was a guest lecturer and a major presenter for the O'More Image Conservatory each semester. I find Ms. Bumgarner to be a superb speaker and writer, with excellent interaction skills in the classroom. She has much to offer with her unique and practical style of teaching about image and style, a subject for which she has much knowledge and experience."
Dr. K. Mark Hilliard, Vice Chancellor and President, The Hilliard Institute

"Lori has fresh eyes and vision, and she shares with clients what to expect in the industry. *Advance Your Image* has been a key resource for the Image Conservatory I oversee."
Karol Lahrman, Owner, Reflection Model and Talent Agency

Second Edition

Advance Your Image

Putting your best foot forward never goes out of style.

by Lori Bumgarner

Advance Your Image

Copyright ©2009, 2010 by Lori Bumgarner,
paNASH Style, www.paNASHstyle.com.

ISBN 13 978-0-9846244-2-3
ISBN 10 0-9846244-2-2

Special thanks to Mike Coleman and Nicole Masullo
for proofreading and editing.
Cover photo from iStockphoto.
Author photo by Van Dresser Studios.
Randy Shreve photo by Van Dresser Studios.
Braden Gray photo by Anthony Scarlati.
Brittany McLamb photo by Tony Denning Photo.

Second Edition Book Block Design by Whitnee Clinard.
Illustration Design and Drawings by Anastasia Morozova.

Second Edition Published by:
Hilliard Press
A Division of The Hilliard Institute
Franklin, Tennessee
Oxford, England
www.hilliardinstitute.com

This publication is designed to provide competent and reliable information regarding the subject matter covered. The author specifically disclaims any liability that is incurred from the use or application of the contents of this book.

First and foremost I want to thank my Heavenly Father whom I relied on from the beginning for the direction of this book. Every chapter was prayed over before it was written, and I could not have created it without my Creator's inspiration and strength.

I am also forever grateful to my family—including my father Olin, my sister Susan, and my brother Nelson—for their love and continued support. To my second family—my closest and dearest friends including Danielle Wofford and Sherry Massaro—I thank you for your encouragement and words of wisdom.

Thanks to my colleagues including Dr. Denisha Bonds, Dr. Mark Hilliard, and Jessa Sexton for believing in this book and to the O'More Publishing Company for taking my idea to the next level. Thank you to Mike Coleman, Nicole Masullo, illustrator Anastasia Morozova, designer Whitnee Webb, my wonderful clients, and the many photographers who helped bring my words to life.

And a final thanks to my readers. Thank you for taking the time to follow my blog and for reading this book. I hope you learn something new, refer to it often, and enjoy a new level of confidence as you put its principles to practice!

To my beautiful mother Barbara...I miss you.

Table of Contents

Preface

When I was young girl, one year for Christmas my grandmother gave me a set of Tomy Toys' Fashion Plates. From then on I knew I wanted to be a fashion designer when I grew up. Well, that never quite worked out because my sketching skills were not exactly up to par, and my sewing skills were nonexistent. What I was good at was first as a child dressing my Barbie dolls in their various fashions and then as I got older dressing and styling my friends. But there was a lot that happened between my Barbie days and my current styling days.

My career goals changed when I got to college at UNC Charlotte and majored in my favorite subject of psychology, all while working on campus in the provost's office and serving as a student orientation leader. I loved working in the setting of a college campus and enjoyed helping the new students adjust to college life. I enjoyed it so much that I thought, "How can I continue to help college students even after I've graduated?" After inquiring with my dean of students on how to get a job like his, I learned I would need a master's degree in higher education administration. So, immediately after undergrad I officially became a Gamecock at the University of South Carolina in their nationally-ranked higher education administration master's program.

Gaining experience in various areas of college programming through internships and other hands-on experience helped me determine that career counseling was the specific area of higher education administration that I wanted to pursue. Once I became a college career advisor, I enjoyed using my God-given spiritual gift of encouragement to build confidence in students who were embarking on the exciting journey into "the real world." I taught them to embrace career exploration, be open to new opportunities, and pursue their passions.

While I thrived for ten years in the beautifully landscaped setting of a college campus and loved working with college students who kept me young at heart, I couldn't help but notice all the other exciting job opportunities that cross a career advisor's desk on a daily basis. So, I decided to follow my own advice and found a way to combine my early interests of fashion and styling, my love of music, and my passion for helping people realize their career goals. While still working full-time in the Career Center at Vanderbilt University here in Nashville, Tennessee, I began spending my free time doing research to see what I needed to do to start my own business as an image consultant, wardrobe stylist, and media coach for recording artists and others. I put to test the skills I had taught my students and pounded the pavement by networking with numerous people in the Nashville music and fashion industries. Nine months later, I took a leap of faith and left my secure job with benefits to focus full-time on my company paNASH Style. That was two months before the economy tanked in the fall of 2008, and while it's been a slow, arduous process, I have not regretted my decision.

I love how my past experience of job interview coaching fits in so nicely with my work in providing media interview coaching for my recording artists and how my eye for style allows me to be so creative when developing my clients' image. It's especially rewarding to build confidence in new artists who are just on the cusp of success, much like it was in helping my college students venturing into the real world, but different in so many ways.

The principles used in working with my recording artists are ones that readers from all walks of life will be able to apply to their own efforts in improving their image. It is my hope that *Advance Your Image* will build in all readers the confidence and courage to dig down deep and polish the gem that they already are so they can shine even brighter!

Lori Bumgarner

Introduction

I'm not much of a collector. There are only two things I really collect: shoes and inspirational quotes. As you read this book, you'll see that I've started each chapter with one of my favorite quotes that explains what I'm trying to convey in that particular chapter.

We've all heard the quote "image is everything!" (Note: this is not one of my favorite quotes.) But have you ever asked yourself why image is so important? Why does it make a difference? Shouldn't talent, skills, and abilities matter more than image? The purpose of this book is to not only provide the answers to these questions, but also to help you view yourself with a different lens and to show you how to develop your image in order to maximize opportunities to demonstrate your talents, skills, and abilities. While some of the information you'll find here will not be anything you haven't already read or heard before, it is my hope that all of this information will help you build your confidence in a way that will make you shine, so people will want to know more about what you have to offer the world.

You may be an aspiring recording artist trying to make a name for yourself, a job seeker going through a career transition, or a busy mom in need of personal attention. Whatever your situation, you may feel that you are in need of a change but aren't sure how to get started. Improving your image is one of the best ways to invest in your future, boost your confidence, and enhance your life both professionally and personally. Having a positive image of yourself has a tremendous effect on your human trinity: your mind, body, and soul. In this book, you will learn how to present yourself in the best possible light by looking and feeling your best and by communicating your strengths and uniqueness in every possible way, whether it is in person, online, or on paper.

It is my ministry to help people jump-start their professional goals, achieve their career goals, and feel good and positive about themselves and their current situations in their professional and personal lives. God has provided me the education, experience, skills, creativity, and desire to do so. My ten years experience as a career advisor has paved the way for me to best teach you how to sell yourself to your audience, supporters, potential employers, potential clients, and others through professional resumes and biographies, networking strategies, interviews, and more. My lifelong passion and eye for fashion and style gives me the ability to help you come up with the best look for you that makes you stand taller and complements your body, your personality, your talent, and your career goals.

What I am providing you in the following pages is what I have learned over the years in serving a variety of people: college students entering the workforce for the first time, military personnel making the transition into civilian work, people going through significant career changes or transitions, entertainers learning how to promote themselves through the media, recording artists developing their image, and more.

Advance Your Image begins with the importance of image in Chapter 1 and how to polish your look in Chapter 2. Polishing your look includes starting with what you have (your current clothing and your current body type), updating your look, and paying attention to the details and adding the finishing touches. Chapter 3 discusses how to make yourself look good even when you are not visible to others. This includes helping you look good on paper in your resume and/or your biography and helping you look good in your online persona. Your online presence is a part of your image, and you have to know how to properly present yourself in your online tools such as social and professional networking sites. Finally, in Chapters 4 and 5, *Advance Your Image* teaches you how to best present yourself in a variety of in-person situations including networking events, job interviews, meetings, media interviews, etc.

As you read *Advance Your Image* and work through the Appendix, start thinking about what steps you can take to improve your image. As you take these steps, also take note of how others are responding to you. Are you getting noticed in a good way instead of being overlooked or being noticed in a bad way? Are you getting more compliments from people on your appearance and your disposition? Are you experiencing favor in ways you've never experienced before? When you start taking pride in yourself and your image, people start to take notice and take an interest in you and what you have to offer the world. Putting your best foot forward never goes out of style!

Lori Bumgarner

Chapter 1

What is Image?

"We must radiate success before it will come to us."
Earl Nightingale

"Image is everything!" You may be asking yourself, what is the "everything" of image? This chapter will outline all that "everything" includes. First, image is NOT just your physical appearance, and it is NOT about being vain or conceited.

Image is defined as
  • "a mental picture or impression of something;"
  • "a mental conception held in common by members of a group and symbolic of a basic attitude and orientation;" or
  • "a popular conception (as of a person, institution, or nation) projected especially through the mass media."

As you can see from these definitions found in *Webster's Dictionary*, our image includes our attitude, our orientation, and others' perceptions of us. These things obviously go deeper than our physical appearance. Our image is a combination of our own various characteristics that we project to others and others' perceptions of those characteristics. Those characteristics include our physical appearance (how our clothes, hair, skin, and body looks), our communication skills (how we speak to and listen to others and how we write), and our behavior (how we connect with others and how we promote ourselves).

When it comes to our physical appearance, people make judgments and assumptions about us within the first seven seconds they lay their eyes on us. Is this fair? Of course not! Is it reality? Of course it is! We are all guilty of taking one look at people and making an assumption about them: what kind of work they may do, where they may be coming from or where they may be on their way to, how old they may be, what their socio-economic status is, where they are from, etc.

When considering this, there are two questions you must ask yourself:

  • "Do I care what others think about how I look?" The fact that you are reading this book tells me that you probably do care.
  • "What kind of image do I want to project?" Your answer to this question may vary depending on the various roles in your life.

Advance Your Image

We all play various roles in our lives: son or daughter, friend, sibling, spouse, parent, employee, supervisor, volunteer, coach, etc. The list goes on and on. Depending on your role and your situation at any given time, you will need an image that is appropriate to that role and situation. While there are some people who go through life thinking they can have a "one-size-fits-all" look for all aspects of their lives, most people realize the need for attire that is appropriate for a variety of events and situations. For example, recording artists develop a physical image through their wardrobe that is appropriate for the variety of given situations they face in their careers. There is a certain look they need to have when they are performing on a stage, when they are in a photo shoot or a video shoot, when they are attending an awards show, when they are meeting with label executives, when they are making television appearances, and even when they are trying to maintain their privacy.

Knowing your audience

As the third definition of the term "image" states, your image is something that is projected to others, especially the mass media. Even if you are not in the public eye, you need to know who your audience is. If you are a recording artist, you need to know who your demographic is, how you relate to that demographic, and what that demographic responds to. If you are a real estate agent, you need to know who your clientele is, how you relate with them, and how they respond to you. By having this knowledge, you will be able to answer the question of what kind of image you want to project.

With the help of an image consultant, you will learn how to create a look that
- is consistent with the image you want to project to your audience;
- will make you more approachable; and
- will help you convey competence, exude confidence, and command respect.

Once you have a more confident and approachable appearance pulled together, you will notice increased opportunities to connect and communicate with others and expand your audience. This means you will be communicating with people more than you probably ever have

Lori Bumgarner

before, both personally and professionally. If you are in a high-profile profession and you look the part, you will be seen as an expert or "star" in your chosen profession and will be called on to share your story and expertise in front of an audience or through the media, including print, radio, or television. Therefore, your next step in improving your image includes honing your communication and listening skills to articulate what it is you do and to appropriately answer questions about yourself.

Promoting yourself

It is your job to sell yourself in your communication with others because no one else will! And besides, would you really want someone other than yourself selling you? Some people may answer "yes" to that question because their confidence is so low that they can't see all the talent, abilities, skills, and other great qualities they possess. But one thing as an image consultant I can guarantee: if you *look* like you've got the skills and talent, people will believe you have the skills and talent, and they will then notice those strengths and will compliment you on them. The more you hear those compliments, the more you start to believe them, and the more you start to demonstrate those strengths.

The more you put yourself in situations to communicate with others, the better and more natural you will become at promoting yourself in a genuine way that will make you likeable and approachable. Promoting yourself and what you do is not the same thing as being a braggart or a "show-boater." Remember, your communication skills also include how well you listen. Taking the time to listen to others before talking about yourself will show your genuine interest in them and endear you to them. Listening to and caring about what others have to say will build trust, allowing people to take you more seriously.

Expanding your network is much more than introducing yourself to 20 people at a conference and exchanging business cards. In Chapter 4, I will discuss networking and what it involves. When done properly, networking can lead to great success regardless of your profession or industry. When you are networking, you're projecting an image of yourself, hopefully the right image of you!

Advance Your Image

When it comes to image, sometimes you make that first impression in writing long before you have a chance to make a first impression in person. This can happen in several possible ways. If you are a recording artist, your bio and blogs on social networking sites may be read before your music is heard. Also, potential fans may read about you in an interview you've done with a magazine before they've become familiar with your music. If you are a job seeker, usually it is an email message, cover letter, and/or resume that your potential employers see before meeting you in person. Job seekers must also be careful about what they post in blogs and on their social networking site profiles since more and more employers are reviewing candidates' online presence when making hiring decisions. It is my guess that this practice will become an illegal hiring practice (just like making hiring decisions based on age, marital status, and other personal information) in the near future. However, this has not yet happened, so be careful what you put out there in cyberspace for everyone to see. How you present yourself in writing can make or break your reader's decision to get to know you more.

Once you understand all that is involved in your image and the importance of projecting the right image to your audience, you can begin taking the necessary steps to improve and polish your image to achieve your goals.

Lori Bumgarner

Chapter 2

Polishing Your Look

"Fashion can be bought. Style one must possess."
Edna Woolman Chase

What is style?

Let me state up-front that having style is not about being extravagant, being a "label whore," or being obsessed with the latest trends or fads. Having style is more about possessing good taste and knowing what's right for your body, your personality, and your lifestyle, regardless of the amount on the price tag. This is why I love this quote from Edna Woolman Chase, former editor-in-chief of *Vogue*. Even if people have millions to spend on new clothes, shoes, and bags, they may still lack an eye for what works for their body type, their lifestyle, and their career goals.

Generally speaking, there are two types of fashion offenders in this world, those who don't put any thought into their clothing or looks, and those who over-think their clothing and looks. We've all seen or known both types of "fashionably challenged" people. Within each of those two groups there are two more groups:

- Unconsciously incompetent – the ones who don't know they have poor fashion sense (the ones who will probably never read this book).
- Consciously incompetent – the ones who know they have poor fashion sense and want to improve it but don't know how, don't have the time, or are at a certain point in their lives that they are waiting for something else to happen before they start trying to improve their appearance.

My goal as an image consultant is to teach the consciously incompetent to become either consciously competent (learning good fashion sense and work at maintaining it) or unconsciously competent (developing a fashion sense that becomes second nature to them). In the process of teaching those folks how to develop their own style, it is my hope that the unconsciously incompetent will take notice and decide that they want to look their best as well. I would be lying if I said I didn't want to help the unconsciously incompetent. Of course I do! But I can only help those who want to be helped.

Common concerns

One of the most common excuses I hear from people who are hesitant about improving their image is they want to lose weight first before going out and buying new clothes. First let me say, congratulations to those of you who have set that goal and are working hard toward it! Now, let me ask you a question: why should you have to wait to start looking and feeling good when you can start doing so right now? You are never too heavy to be fashionable.

I understand that you may have a fear that if you find clothes you like right now, you won't be motivated to lose the weight. It's actually quite the opposite, however. When you start dressing your body better now, people will think you've already started to lose weight because wearing clothing that's flattering to your current body type gives the illusion of looking thinner. Compliments and encouragement from others actually motivate you even more to lose the weight, and you are therefore more successful at achieving your goal than if you were to put off dressing better. You might as well indulge yourself in the pleasure of shopping since you can't indulge yourself with your favorite foods while on a diet and exercise program. And you can indulge in clothing without having to spend a lot of money.

Imagine it this way: if you had a painful injury that you had to wait three months for a surgery to heal it, and the doctor told you that there was an affordable medication that is safe and has no side effects you can take for the next three months to minimize your pain while you are waiting for the surgery, would you opt to take the medicine, or would you choose to walk around in pain everyday for three months? You would probably choose to take the medication.

You're worth looking good right now! You don't want to be passed up when the right opportunity comes along because you are putting your image and appearance on hold. Besides, looking your best has a tremendous positive effect on your human trinity (your mind, body, and soul) which will in turn attract others to you. You are already beautiful on the inside, so let it show on the outside!

Lori Bumgarner

Improving your appearance

There are two main things that you can start doing now to improve your appearance. First, wear clothes that fit you properly. You will look slimmer if you wear clothes that fit than if you wear clothes that are too big or too small for you. If you already have some great clothes that just need to be slightly altered for a perfect fit, then invest the money to have that done. Tailoring what you already have is often less expensive than buying an entire new wardrobe. Not only will you look slimmer, your clothes will also look more expensive! Wearing ill-fitting clothes is one of the biggest fashion offenses that occur today. Men tend to wear clothes that are too big, and women tend to wear clothes that are too tight or too small. Either mistake will make you look heavier than you are. Philip Dormer Stanhope was noted for saying, "His clothes fit him so ill, and constrain him so much, that he seems rather their prisoner than their proprietor." Wear what flatters and works with your body, not what you wish you look good in.

Ladies, look for garments that accentuate your curves and avoid those that create a boxy look. Also, don't be afraid to have a little fun with your outfit by adding a funky or fierce shoe that will make you stand taller and feel powerful. Finally, make sure your hair style complements and frames your face and brings life and a little bit of edge to your look.

Advance Your Image

Blending classics with trends.

Lori Bumgarner

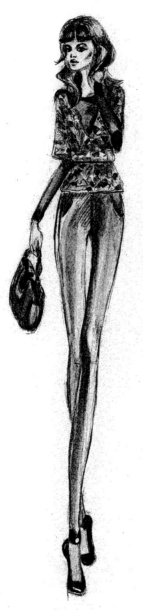

Age-appropriate fashions for women: 20s

Age-appropriate fashions for women: 30s

Advance Your Image

Second, wear clothing that is age appropriate. Wearing clothing that is too young for you will make you look just as old as wearing clothing that is too mature for you. On that same note, wearing clothing that is out-of-date will also age you. You need to wear up-to-date styles and fashions without giving in to the latest fads. There is a difference between fads, trends, and fashions. It is smart to mix a few modern trends with some timeless classics. Getting stuck in a time warp is another common mistake I see among the fashionably challenged. Wearing the same clothes and styles that you wore ten years ago in college will not make you look like you are twenty years old again. Instead, it will make you look ten years older than you actually are (or if you're a musician you'll look like you're still in a garage band)! It's time to throw out those clothes and hire an image consultant who will help you find the look you need that complements your current life roles and career goals while still reflecting your personality and interests.

Updating your image

Speaking of throwing out old clothes, the first step in updating your image is to start in your own closet. First, go through and get rid of items that are outdated, stained, damaged beyond repair, and no longer fit. Make sure you don't just throw these items in the trash. Instead, take the salvageable items to your local clothing donation center. Next, before getting rid of items that you haven't worn in more than a year—especially the ones that still have tags on them—you need to start putting together new outfits with what's left in your closet. It is this part of the closet clean-out where most people need assistance because they don't realize all the possible combinations that are lying dormant in their closets.

One of my favorite things in my career as an image consultant is helping my clients save money by creating new outfits from their current wardrobe. This is done by pairing separates, jackets, shoes, and accessories together in ways that clients would have never previously considered. Those items that have been sitting in your closet with the tags still on them will finally find their place in the rest of your wardrobe. "Shopping" in your own closet is one of several ways to get more bang for your buck. You will have several new outfits without ever spending a dime on new clothing!

Lori Bumgarner

Age-appropriate fashions for women: 40s

Age-appropriate fashions for women: 50s

Advance Your Image

Starting in your closet can also help you save money when you head out to department stores and boutiques. By starting in your closet, you can determine what you really need and make a list of the necessary items missing from your current wardrobe. Having a list in hand when heading to the stores will prevent you from making impulse purchases on items you don't need.

Next, you are ready for the fun part of updating your wardrobe—shopping for new items! When you are ready for this next step, keep these additional money-saving tips in mind:

- Don't buy anything that doesn't feel right! If there is something about an article of clothing that gives you some type of reservation when you try it on, don't waste your time or money trying to determine where you will wear it or if you will fit into it after you lose the weight. Take it off and move on.
- Don't buy anything that doesn't go with at least three things in your closet. For instance, if you need to purchase a new suit for a job interview, make sure that the different pieces can be mixed and matched with other pieces in your closet. This is easier to determine if you shop in your own closet before you head to the stores because you will have a better idea of what you already actually own.
- Avoid shopping for yourself during holidays. Shopping during the holiday season is hectic, and shoppers are easily distracted. Holiday shopping often leads to impulse buying. Also, your weight is likely to fluctuate during this time of year.
- Be mindful of spending money on trends. One way to update your wardrobe without spending a lot of money is to purchase a few trendy accessories, such as a couple pieces of trendy jewelry or a scarf, and mix those in with your current clothing items. And speaking of trends, while we've all heard the advice to invest in classic, timeless pieces of clothing for your wardrobe, this does not apply to those who get bored easily or those who work in a trendy industry such as the music and entertainment industries. If you like to stay on the cutting edge of fashion, you probably won't get enough wear out of a timeless piece. The thing to remember if you are going to keep up with the trends is to never pay full retail for

Lori Bumgarner

every trend. Also, spend less on garments in trendy colors that will soon be out of style. Remember 80s teal and 90s hunter green? Instead, invest in classic colors such as camel, true red, basic black, etc. It's always good to mix trendy pieces with classic pieces to keep from looking like one big walking fad.

• Pay attention to the care labels. If you don't have extra money for dry cleaning, don't let the majority of your purchases be "dry clean only" items. But here's a little secret: if the care label says "dry clean only" it has to be professionally cleaned, but if the label just says "dry clean" you can usually clean the item yourself at home by hand washing it or washing it in the gentle cycle and letting it line dry.

• Put it on hold! When you are shopping at multiple stores, put the items you have decided upon on hold until you have visited all the other stores you plan to visit. Then go back and settle up at the end of your shopping day. This gives you time to decide if what you have chosen is really a need or an impulse buy.

• Know the store's return policy before buying. At stores and boutiques whose refund policies are "all sales final" or "exchange only," be very selective on your purchases at those stores. Make sure the items you purchase are what you consider to be "must haves."

• Don't sign up for store credit cards. It may be tempting to get that extra 10% off your purchase by signing up for the store credit card, but it's not worth it. If you sign up for more than one of these cards within a six month time period, it will go against you on your credit report.

• Shop consignment. There are so many wonderful consignment stores where you can find some real gems at a fraction of the cost! Many people take items they've only worn once to consignment shops. Most consignment stores have very strict policies on what type of clothing they will accept, so you can be assured that what you are buying is in good condition. While most consignment shops only carry women's clothing, there are a select few that also carry men's clothing.

You will also want to follow these additional shopping tips to ensure a stress-free shopping day:

Advance Your Image

Age-appropriate fashions for men: 20s and 30s

Age-appropriate fashions for men: 40s and 50s

Lori Bumgarner

- Take ONE trusted, honest friend with you. Make sure it's the friend who's not going to hold back about how you look in something. You need a buffer between you and the sales person. An image consultant will not only be honest with you about what doesn't look good on you, but will also find for you the items that do look best on you and will serve as a buffer between you and the sales person. Avoid taking more than one person shopping with you if you are on a mission to do some real shopping. Having too many people and too many opinions can cause confusion and frustration. Save your shopping with a group of girlfriends for times when you're just browsing or window shopping.

- Shop on Tuesdays and Thursdays. Tuesdays are when new merchandise usually arrives at stores. Thursdays are usually when weekend sales start. You'll get the same deals but without having to fight the weekend crowds.

- Shop for shoes in the afternoon. Your feet swell in the afternoon to their largest size so this is the best time to find the right fit for shoes.

- Wear comfortable shoes and clothing that you can get in and out of easily.

- If you can't find your size in an item, ask the sales person if your size might be on one of the mannequins. If so, it's perfectly okay to ask the sales person to remove that item and allow you to buy it provided it is not damaged from the display.

- Don't pay attention to the size number. A size 6 in one store or by one designer is not necessarily the same size as a 6 by another store or designer. That's why it's always best to try on three different sizes to find the perfect fit: your actual size, one size smaller, and one size larger. Don't let the number on the label affect how you feel about yourself.

Finishing touches

Getting new clothes does not complete the task of updating your look. You now have to add the finishing touches. Without these finishing touches, you'll just look undone in your new clothes. For men, details include the right shoes, belts, glasses, and in some cases, jewelry. For male recording artists, there are certain accessories that make a statement and can illustrate your musical style. While we have a growing population of "metrosexuals" (heterosexual men who take an immense amount of pride in their appearance including getting manicures and eyebrow waxing), there are still many men who are hesitant to try men's jewelry or a new hairstyle for fear that it will affect their masculinity. A good image consultant can help a man find the right accessories he is comfortable with and that complement his personality and career goals, such as a briefcase for a business man or a unique necklace for a recording artist to wear on stage or in a photo shoot. Sometimes it's just a matter of updating your look with a current hairstyle or modern frames for glasses.

BEFORE   AFTER

If you wear glasses, a new pair of frames can take years off your face. It's important to up-date your frames every 3 to 5 years so that your look doesn't become dated. Get someone who knows what he or she is doing to help you determine the best frame for your facial shape. With a new pair of glasses, not only will you see sharper, you'll look sharper!

If you haven't updated either in the last three to five years, it's time to do so!

While men tend to under-accessorize, some women tend to over-accessorize because of all the choices they have. Coco Chanel always had a great rule of thumb: remove one accessory before walking out the door. While female recording artists and entertainers can get away with more accessories than most women, not all women should try this.

Lori Bumgarner

Women can use trendy accessories as an inexpensive way to update their wardrobe. Also, the various colors in an accessory can help you pull together an outfit that includes clothing in colors you would have never considered putting together before. One thing you want to avoid most of all is being too "matchy-matchy." You don't want all of your accessories to be the same color as your clothing. Also, I don't recommend buying an earring and necklace set unless you wear the necklace with a different pair of earrings and vice versa. Wearing both together is too "matchy-matchy." In fact, when it comes to shoes, they don't have to match your clothes, they just have to go. Shoes look best when they are a different but complementary color to your outfit. That's when they really stand out and get noticed! When it comes to accent colors, you only want that accent color to show in no more than three accessories.

When putting together new outfits both with the contents of your closet and with newly store-bought garments and accessories, you will find it helpful to use the "Garment

Modern accessories for women.

Modern accessories for men.

Advance Your Image

Review Form" located in the Appendix at the end of this book. This is a page I have designed for you to make copies of for each outfit or article of clothing so you can keep track of the various combinations it can be worn with, when you've worn it, when it was last dry cleaned, and more. Another great resource to help you keep track of your wardrobe is the *Memory Clothes Planner* which can be purchased at www.memoryclothesplanner.com.

Hair and makeup

Okay, before we move on to the topic of women's hairstyles, let me first get this off my chest: while I know that a woman's hair is her crowning glory, it is just hair. Some women are too afraid to cut their hair, even if it will make them look better and younger. Hair grows back. My mother's hair grew back after she lost it all to chemotherapy. During her therapy, she had a sense of humor about it, and if she got hot with her wig on, she would just jerk her wig off and didn't care what other people thought. When her hair grew back after her therapy, it grew back fuller, darker, and more beautiful than ever. My mother had always looked ten years younger than her actual age, but she looked *twenty* years younger when her hair grew back into a cute new short do!

Now, having said that, here are a few rules (not just suggestions) when it comes to completing your look with the right hairstyle.

- Rule #1: long hair does not always equal beautiful or sexy. Some people just can't pull off really long hair, either because it's not flattering to their facial shape, or its texture is too fine for long styles. Get a professional opinion about whether or not you should go to a medium or short length.
- Rule #2: if you've had the same hairstyle for three years or longer, it's time for a change, even if it's just a slight change. I'm talking about the style here, not the color. Think of your hair as an accessory, and change it up every once in a while.
- Rule #3: not every hair has to be in place. You don't want your hair to look contrived or overdone.

Lori Bumgarner

• Rule #4: make sure your hair color complements your skin tone and you maintain the color.

It's important to update your hairstyle to one that best compliments the shape of your face. This goes for both men and women. While many women tend to change their hair more often, many men often keep the same hairstyle for years and even decades. Being open to a new style, even if it is only slightly different, will have a tremendous impact not only on how you look but also how you feel.

When it comes to makeup, you can experiment and have a lot of fun with it because if you don't get it right the first time, you can wash it off and start all over. Always remember, though, that less is more and that makeup is supposed to enhance your look, not transform you into someone who is virtually unrecognizable. Avoid outdated makeup techniques such as matching your eye shadow to your outfit. Use highlighter on your cheekbones and on the inside corners of your eyes, and people will comment on your beautiful glow!

Remember, your best accessory is your smile! Your smile should always be a genuine smile which is one where you are smiling not only with your mouth but also with your eyes. With your new polished look, you will have greater confidence that will keep you smiling!

Chapter 3

Looking Good on Paper (and Online!)

"It is better to write a bad first draft than
to write no first draft at all."
Will Shetterly

Your image is not just about how you look physically. It also involves how you look on paper. There will be times in your life and your career when you will have to promote yourself in writing, whether it's in a resume or cover letter, in a press release or bio, or on various online social networking sites. When it comes to writing, the hardest part is always getting started. This chapter will help you get your thoughts together for promoting yourself in writing and will cover several writing dos and don'ts.

Bios

Let's first start with your bio. Almost everyone needs a bio. Recording artists and musicians need one for their web sites and press kits, and professionals and business owners need one for their company web sites and proposals. For a recording artist, you need to bring your fans into your experience with you. Let them get to know the real you. Start with where you are currently in your career and work backwards in your history. While your bio should always be written in the third person, you still need to make it come alive with descriptions that entice the senses so the reader can feel as if he or she is right there with you. Include your sense of humor to make your bio more attention-grabbing, and always avoid using clichés. When sending a bio to the media, provide them with a shorter, more concise version of your bio. For other professionals, you also want to write your bio in the third person, but it may make more sense for you to write your bio in chronological order. Include your credentials, any presentations or publications, and your involvement in professional associations.

Regardless of your profession or industry, you must make sure your bio is free of any misspellings and grammatical errors. There is no excuse for not proofreading your bio and making necessary corrections. Any mistake can lead the reader to unfair judgments. Mistakes can make the reader question your professionalism and your ability. Any text you put out there for the world to see needs to be free of error. This includes all the text sections of your social networking site profiles and your blogs. Only in tweets and other items with limited characters are you allowed to use abbreviated spelling, but try to keep that to a minimum. You want to avoid writing like you do in your text messages. In fact, if you take the time to use correct spelling and grammar, you will stand out from others, and people will respect you for your professionalism. If you are the type who has stronger skills in areas other than writing, hire an editor to help you keep up with your blogs and help you proof and edit your other written material.

Online presence

When it comes to your image and the Internet, you must make sure you have a "clean" online presence. One wrong thing ending up on the Internet can permanently tarnish your image and damage your reputation and career. Some things to remember when posting information about yourself online include the following:

- Occasionally Google yourself and see what comes up. If you find something that casts you in a bad light, take all necessary action to get it removed.
- Remove questionable material from all your online profiles.
- Ask your friends to remove any questionable photos or content they may have of you on their own profile pages.
- Educate yourself on the privacy policies of each site on which you post a profile.
- Be selective of who you approve as a friend on your page.
- Complete the "Online Self-Audit" located in the Appendix on pages 80 through 82.

Following these guidelines will help you maintain a positive online presence.

Resumes

One of the most important documents you will need for your career is a professional resume. There are four things you need to know about resumes:

- There is not just one correct way to write a resume.

- A resume is not something you can sit down and write in one hour, one night, or even one week. It takes numerous revisions to be letter perfect and will always be a work in progress.
- Employers or recruiters will spend only ten seconds looking at your resume the first time they view it.
- The purpose of a resume is not to get you the job but to get you the job interview. It is also used as a credential in promoting yourself for things other than just interviews, such as a credential for your speaking engagements and more.

Regardless of your reasons for needing a resume, like all your other written material it too should be letter perfect and completely free of errors. Since recruiters are bombarded with resumes, they look for reasons to throw out your resume instead of reasons to keep it. Misspellings, grammatical errors, and inconsistencies in format are just a few of the reasons they throw out resumes. That's why it's important to follow these tips on making your resume stand out above the competition:

- Be specific in your objective statement, or just leave it out. You don't necessarily need an objective statement on your resume, especially if you don't have room to put one without going over one or two full pages. If you decide to include an objective statement, it cannot be vague. It must specifically state the job and company with which you are applying. That's it. No more. No philosophical statement about how you are going to save the world with your skills.
- Make your resume easy to read. Avoid writing in paragraph form. List your duties using concise bulleted statements. Show what you have to offer when listing your past job duties by including the results you garnered from your efforts. This is most important in developing your resume! Keep your resume targeted to the position for which you are applying. You don't have to include every job you've ever had. Only list past jobs relevant to the job you are applying for, and keep it to one or two full pages.
- Avoid listing irrelevant interests. Only list those interests that are relevant to the job or the industry. Don't take up limited space

Advance Your Image

on your resume with irrelevant interests where you can instead emphasize your accomplishments in past jobs. An exception to this rule would be, for example, if you are an avid golfer and the potential job requires you to close deals with clients while taking them out for a day of golf, then it would be beneficial to list a personal interest such as this.

• Make sure your formatting is consistent. If you have your education section heading in bold, then your experience section heading should be in bold. Don't ever give the recruiter an excuse to throw out your resume before having the chance to read it more carefully.

• Get your resume critiqued by a professional. When you've been working on your resume at length, it's easy to miss some mistakes that have been staring you in the face, even if you have proofread it several times. A fresh pair of eyes will catch the mistakes you may have missed. A professional who has numerous years of experience in writing and critiquing resumes can make suggestions on appropriate wording and how to organize your information to target your resume to the job. This will maximize your chances of getting called for an interview.

• Follow the "Resume Guidelines" listed in the Appendix on pages 83 and 84.

Cover letters

A resume should always be accompanied by a well-written cover letter. The purpose of the cover letter is to introduce yourself to the reader, express your interest in the position and indicate how you heard about it, share one or two examples of how you have demonstrated your skills in past experience (including work experience, volunteer experience, committee work, etc.), and ask for the interview. The cover letter should not be a repeat of what's on your resume. It should only be three to four paragraphs in length, and you need to show some assertiveness in the final paragraph by tactfully asking for the opportunity of an interview. Once again, proofread and get professional feedback on your cover letter just as you would for your resume.

Lori Bumgarner

While looking good on paper takes a lot of time, it is well worth the effort because it is a very important part of your brand and your image that you are trying to build. Neglecting this part of your image will make all the work you put into the other parts of your image worthless. Following these guidelines and seeking assistance from experts will help you in developing this part of your image and keeping it well-maintained.

Chapter 4

Making Connections

"You'll always miss 100% of the shots you don't take."
Wayne Gretzky

Currently, there are thousands of books listed on Amazon.com that cover the subject of networking. Everyone has heard how important it is to network and make connections. It is the number one way to get the word out about what you have to offer, whether it's in a job, in your business, or through your talent. How you present yourself, both in your look and your communication skills, can greatly affect both the quantity and the quality of contacts you make throughout your life. Understanding not only the "what" and the "why" of networking but also the "who," the "when," the "where," and the "how" of networking is important. This chapter will cover those areas so that you will learn to network effectively. In addition, the art of networking does not come naturally to everyone, hence the number of books written on the subject to teach people how to network. If you are not comfortable or familiar with the process of making connections and building a network, this chapter will help you learn how to gain confidence and feel more comfortable with the process of building your network.

Who

First, it is important to determine with whom you should be networking. Consider everyone you meet as a possible contact. While the person you meet through your sister's roommate or your uncle's hunting buddy may not be the person in the position to make a difference in your career, it doesn't mean that he or she doesn't know someone who is. If you think about all the people you know, consider how many people each of those folks know, and you can see how your network can grow exponentially! It's always good to sit down and brainstorm a list of all the people you know. Start with the obvious ones such as your relatives and your friends. Then list your neighbors, previous supervisors and co-workers, former classmates, people you know from your church or service organizations, people you've met through your social activities, and so on. You'll see that as you make your list, it will continue to grow and grow!

When

Second, you need to know when to network. While there are many structured networking events held in your chosen industry that you'll want to attend, realize that networking on an informal basis occurs all the time. You never know what event, trip, errand, activity, etc. will turn into a networking opportunity. You can make a connection while visiting a friend in the hospital, attending a wedding, going to a music festival, frequenting a local coffee shop, etc. One thing to remember about when to network is that it should continue at all times: before you start looking for a job, during your job search, and after you've already found a job or achieved your career goals. Since networking is about building relationships, you want to maintain those relationships throughout your lifetime and return the favor to someone who has helped you in the past or pay it forward to someone who is just starting out.

Where

Third, just like every person and every time can be a potential networking opportunity, so can every place. Unintentional networking can occur in just about any place you may be: the bank, the post office, vacation spots, concerts, wine tastings, the gym, social networking sites, etc. It's important to remember to be intentional in your networking as well. You want to target your networking to places where other industry leaders frequent such as industry conferences, industry events, and their favorite lunch restaurants. It's important to do your best to get to know someone in the industry who is well-respected and will invite you to attend these events as their guest.

How

One way to get to know someone like this is through a method of networking called informational interviewing. This method involves setting up a time with or through the contacts you've already made to meet with someone in the industry to discuss their career path and the advice they would have for others trying to break into the industry. Most people are open to doing this because it gives them a chance to help someone, especially if they remember having been helped in the same way when they were first starting out. This is a great way to research an industry in preparation for your career, but it's also a great way to network because one of the questions you always want to ask the person you're interviewing is, "Can you give me the names of two or three other people you think I should talk to?" Start with your contacts, or be bold enough to make some cold calls to set up an informational interview.

Lori Bumgarner

However, before you start reaching out to these folks, you need to have prepared a "mini commercial" of yourself or what some people call "an elevator speech." (In the music and entertainment industries, it's referred to as a "sound bite" or a collection of sound bites.) It's called an elevator speech because it should be brief enough (7-15 seconds) for you to say during the duration of an elevator ride in case you ever find yourself in the elevator (or elsewhere) with someone who can possibly help make or break your career. It should include an introduction of yourself, what you do, and what you have to offer. It should be something that you are so comfortable saying that you can say it in your sleep without sounding rehearsed. This speech is great to use when attending networking events, when calling to set up informational interviews, and when you have to answer the commonly asked interview question, "Can you tell me about yourself?"

An example of a brief elevator speech might sound like this: "Hi! I'm Lori Bumgarner, and I'm an image consultant who helps people put their best foot forward to jump-start their career. I work primarily with recording artists by helping them with wardrobe styling and preparing them for their media interviews. Since I was previously a career advisor for ten years, I also help other people with their resumes and preparation for their job interviews including what to wear for the interview and how to best present their skills in the interview." This kind of introduction piques the listener's curiosity to find out more about *how* you do what you do. Then, you need to be able to expand on that when the listener asks you for more information. Having someone help you script your elevator speech is important because this is the part of your image that is put into action. You can find instructions on how to begin creating your elevator speech in the "Networking Goals" section of the Appendix on page 85.

Meeting contacts through informational interviews can be the beginning of future relationships that you'll want to foster. Remember to return the favor by doing something for the person who agrees to give you the time to interview him or her. This could be as simple as sending a handwritten thank you note or treating him or her to a cup of coffee.

Always be professional and use proper etiquette in your meetings and communications with the people you connect with. Do this by following these networking etiquette tips:

- Do your homework. Don't ask questions in a networking situation such as an informational interview that you could have easily looked up the answers to on your own. Be able to discuss the things going on in the industry by reading industry newsletters and publications on a regular basis.

- Don't act desperate. Desperation can be seen from a mile away, and people are turned off by it. Instead, be positive, show confidence, and smile a genuine smile.

- Don't be a user. Don't try to connect with someone because of only what you hope to get out of the relationship. You never want to ride someone's coat tails or invite yourself to be a part of something. If you have made a good first impression and you are working at developing relationships, people will want to have you around and will invite you to be a part of what they're trying to accomplish.

- Listen. It's true that we were given two ears and one mouth because we need to listen more than we talk. Listen to others and show genuine interest in people instead of thinking about what you want to say when it's your turn to talk. People love to talk about themselves, so ask people questions about their interests and their work.

- Respect your contact's time. If you are at a networking event, don't take up someone else's time by talking only to that person and hogging his or her time. If you have scheduled an informational interview or meeting with someone, stick to the agreed upon time frame.

- Obtain permission. Ask your contact if it's okay that you tell the people he or she has referred you to where you got his or her name. Also, when contacting someone to whom you've been referred, always show that person courtesy by telling that person how you got his or her name. This is not the same thing as name-dropping, which is a no-no.

Lori Bumgarner

•Don't be pushy. Be sensitive to what a contact is willing to do for you, and never push beyond that or expect more.

•Don't make people feel like they're being "networked." This should be especially true at functions that are not specifically designed as networking events.

Networking for the shy

For many people who are either shy or perform better in front of groups instead of communicating one-on-one with others, the thought of networking can be intimidating. However, the more you do it, the more comfortable you become with it, and the more natural it feels. In fact, networking *should* be a natural thing. A lot of it has to do with divine connections and the orchestration of "coincidences" to be at the right place at the right time. That doesn't mean that you shouldn't be strategic in trying to get your name and your purpose out to others. Some of the following tips will help make the process of strategic networking feel more natural to those who are shy when it comes to connecting with new people:

• Treat every networking opportunity as a normal "get-to-know-you" conversation while keeping it professional.

• Start with the people you already know and feel comfortable with. Invite them to go with you to events that will lend to networking opportunities and ask them to introduce you to the people there that they know.

• When friends give you the name of one of their contacts, ask them to let their contact know ahead of time that you will be contacting him or her so that person will have a "heads up" and will know why you are contacting him or her.

• If you are going to make cold calls to industry people, start first by sending them an email or "friending" them on their social or professional networking sites.

• Do your research on the person and his or her project, company, organization, etc. prior to contacting him or her. This will make the conversation flow more smoothly and will show that you have a genuine interest in the person.

- Plan some talking points that you want to cover prior to calling the person.
- Set goals. If you go to an industry event, set a goal to talk to a certain number of new people before you treat yourself to the hors d'oeuvres.

A lot of people object to networking, saying they feel phony in trying to do it and that it feels unnatural. By putting into practice the guidelines listed above, the process will become second nature to you. You will find it easier to approach others, and you will also become more approachable to others.

Wayne Gretzky was right when he said, "You'll always miss 100% of the shots you don't take." Remember that everyone at any place and at any time is a potential connection. Take advantage of every opportunity that comes your way to meet new people. You never know what they may have to offer you and what you may have to offer them.

Lori Bumgarner

Chapter 5

Promoting Yourself

"We all walk in the dark and each of us must learn to
turn on his or her own light."
Earl Nightingale

Your image plays a huge role in the success of your career. Whether you are interviewing for a job, being considered for a record deal, or promoting your single in a media interview, how you present yourself will make a huge difference in the outcome of your meeting. This not only includes your physical appearance or how you're dressed, but also how you sell your best qualities and greatest strengths. Once you've applied the advice from the previous chapters, you're now ready to prepare yourself for the opportunities that await you!

Doing your research

The first and most important step you need to take to impress in a meeting or interview is to DO YOUR RESEARCH! There is no excuse for skipping this step. Conducting research is necessary to:

- show that you are genuinely interested in the opportunity and the company or organization,
- help you respond intelligently to questions and topics of conversation, and
- help you make an informed decision.

Remember, the decision-making process in any business meeting, including interviews, is a two-way street. You need to determine if accepting a job offer or signing a deal with a particular label or organization is the best decision for your career. Conducting research beforehand and asking the right questions will help you make the right decision for you. For recording artists, don't let your excitement that a label has shown interest in you cause you to make a rash decision. The things you should research include:

- the organization's mission and purpose,
- its growth and future goals,
- the current challenges it faces, and
- how your talents and experience fit with the organization and the opportunity at hand.

Advance Your Image

When on a radio tour, recording artists should take the time to do a little research on each radio station and its listener demographic. You can start your research by going through every part of the organization's web site, reading recent press releases from the organization, reading industry trade publications, and talking to others who have been involved in the organization.

Making a good first impression

Going into a meeting or interview equipped with the knowledge and insight you gained from your research will make a good first impression. However, there are additional things that are involved in making a good first impression. Some things to keep in mind: there is something called "The Rule of 12." People remember the first 12 words you speak, the first 12 steps you take, the first 12 inches from the top of your head down, and the first 12 inches of you from the floor up. Also, your message gets across in the following ways:

- 7% is based on the words you use.
- 38% is based on your voice quality.
- 55% is based on your nonverbal cues.

Finally, the information you share with others is retained by listeners in the following ways:

- 4% is retained by touch and smell.
- 11% is retained by hearing.
- 85% is retained by sight.

These statistics change slightly for media interviews such as radio and print, but the rules still apply. Recording artists must remember that their job is to gain the acceptance of not just radio listeners, but also of radio managers so they will add the artists' songs in rotation. Now that you know what you have working for and against you, let's talk about how to take advantage of this knowledge and make it work in your favor.

Lori Bumgarner

To make a good first impression, always start with a positive attitude and a genuine smile. Already have that smile on your face before you even walk in the room, and always leave any negativity at the door. No matter how much negativity you've experienced thus far in the pursuit of your career goals, never let any disappointment, desperation, or bitterness show through on your face or in your voice.

Also, extend a firm handshake. The way you shake hands with others indicates your level of confidence. You are seen as lacking confidence if you hesitate to extend your hand or if your grip is not firm. You are seen as confident if you immediately extend your hand and have the right amount of firmness in your grip. A grip that is overly firm gives the message that you're cocky and egotistical, so practice your handshake with friends, and ask them what they think of it.

In addition, do not take a seat until you have been offered one, maintain good posture, and be aware of your body language. You want to maintain control over any nervous habits you may have. When waiting to be seen, always treat receptionists with respect. Many executives take the opinions of their receptionists seriously and may ask their opinion of you.

Knowing what to wear

Part of making a good first impression is wearing the right thing. Knowing what to wear depends on both the situation (i.e. job interview, label meeting, media interview, performance, etc.) and the industry (i.e. banking, legal, music, etc.). What you would wear to a job interview in a corporation differs greatly from what you would wear to a media interview in the music industry. By doing your research beforehand, you will get an idea of how you should dress for the industry and situation at hand. This involves observing what others who have already made it in that industry wear and by visiting the settings of those people. Find out where they lunch or where they frequent right after work and go there to see how they have dressed for their typical day of hard work. Make sure you also look your best. This might also be a good time and place for you to put into practice some of the networking skills we discussed in Chapter 4.

Advance Your Image

Professional business attire for women.

Lori Bumgarner

Professional business attire for men.

There are some general guidelines that everyone must follow when it comes to dressing for success, regardless of the industry or the career goal. First, you need to make sure that your attire supports your image as someone who takes the opportunity seriously *and* as someone who should also be taken seriously. Notice I said "supports" your image. You don't want your appearance to overpower you as a person. Be remembered for what you say and what you have to bring to the table, not for what you wear. Always try to dress one step above the position for which you are applying. For example, if you are an aspiring recording artist, dress like you are already a star. There are other general guidelines you should follow:

- Looking put together. You never want to look disheveled or sloppy, so make sure that no matter what you are wearing, it is clean and in good condition. Make sure there are no missing buttons or lint on your clothes, and check for dangling threads and tags.

- Looking like a million bucks without spending a million bucks. You don't have to spend a fortune to look the part.

- Wear clothes that fit properly. As I said in Chapter 2, ill-fitting clothes can ruin an entire ensemble.

- Avoid wearing heavy perfume or cologne, and don't go in smelling like cigarettes. You don't want others to have an allergic reaction to how you smell!

- Treat yourself to a manicure (yes, this goes for men too!).

Advance Your Image

Business casual attire for women   Business casual attire for men

Lori Bumgarner

Appropriate media interview attire for male and female recording artists.

Advance Your Image

- When it comes to a corporate job interview, always err on the side of conservative if you're unsure about what you should wear. For instance, many women wonder if they should wear a skirted suit or if they can wear a pant suit. If you're unsure of what the current employees wear, then wear a skirted suit.
- Women should remember they have more room for error than men when it comes to dressing for success since their clothing is often more trendy and flashy.
- Understand what business casual is and is not. Business casual does not mean shorts, sleeveless tanks, mini-skirts, or flip-flops. It can sometimes mean jeans, but only if they are a dark wash jean dressed up with nice shoes and a nice jacket and they are acceptable in that particular setting. This type of look can be a good look for networking at luncheon events or after-work happy hours.
- Seek the help of an image consultant or a well-dressed friend in the industry to help you find just the right outfit.

These rules apply even if you are a recording artist being interviewed on the radio. Many radio stations have a web cam in their studios where they will stream your in-studio visit on their web site, so, yes, you will be seen!

Preparing for commonly asked questions

One of the first questions you will get in just about any introductory meeting or interview is, "Can you tell me about yourself?" This may seem like a very simple question that you wouldn't have to spend much time preparing an answer for since nobody knows you better than you, but once faced with that question, most people freeze up. They get that deer-caught-in-headlights look because, since there is so much they know about themselves, they don't know where to begin. People usually start rambling on about irrelevant information such as where they were born, how many siblings they have, and what their first pet's name was. This is how *not* to answer that first question!

If you have developed an elevator speech as we discussed in Chapter 4, you are already prepared to provide the type of answer the interviewer is

Lori Bumgarner

seeking from you. Your answer should always focus on your professional self, especially if the setting is a job interview. This means you briefly indicate your skills, strengths, and talents along with your past work experience. A more personal response may be required if you are a recording artist going into a meeting with a label executive for a potential record deal (further explained in "Guidelines for Meetings With Labels and Music Publishers" in the Appendix on pages 88 through 90) or if you are doing a media interview (further explained in "Guidelines for Media Interviews" in the Appendix on pages 91 through 93). In this situation, you want your listener to know something about you that is personal that others can relate to yet makes you unique. In either case, you want to convey your passion for your calling and your enthusiasm for the opportunity at hand. While you should always follow the lead of the interviewer, you can somewhat control the course of the interview by briefly mentioning things about yourself in this answer that will pique the interviewer's interest enough to want to ask you more about that topic.

Another commonly asked question is, "What are your greatest strengths?" When answering this question, first listen to how the question is being asked. Did they say "strengths" plural, or did they say "strength" singular? Always answer the question the way it is being asked —only give one strength if asked for only one strength. When giving your answer, always include one example of how you have demonstrated that strength in a past situation. Providing examples to illustrate your response is always necessary to keep from speaking in generalities. Examples are also important in media interviews so your audience can feel like they know you a little bit better as a person and are connected to you.

Sometimes the above question can become a two-part question, "What are your greatest strengths AND greatest weaknesses?" Everyone hates the "weaknesses" question, but the motivation behind it is not what most people usually think it is. This question is not asked to try to make you look bad. Instead, it's asked to help the organization determine where you might need some assistance or additional training on the job. Of course, you don't want to indicate a weakness that would prevent you from getting an offer, such as having a weakness in one of the key responsibilities of that job. If you do have that kind of weakness, you shouldn't be wasting their time or yours for that matter. Instead, indicate a legitimate weakness and follow it up with a positive by either giving an example of how you've compensated for that weakness in the past or how you are currently working to overcome that weakness. Avoid giving the "I'm too much of a perfectionist" canned answer that everybody uses because interviewers can see straight through that answer. This common interview question may be a second part of a two-part question like I mentioned earlier, or it can be a stand-alone question. Remember for any two-part questions to always answer all parts of the question without having to be reminded to do so.

Also expect to be asked, "What do you know about us?" This question is asked in order to determine if you've taken the time to do your research on the organization. If you haven't done that research previously discussed in this chapter, you are sending the message that you're just not interested in or enthusiastic about the opportunity. You send this same message when they ask you, "Do you have any questions for us?" and you have none prepared. Interviewing is a two-way street, and you need to determine if this is the right opportunity and fit for you before you ever make any decision to sign onto something. Avoid asking questions that you can easily find the answers to yourself through your own research. Instead, ask questions that will help you determine if this is where you want to be. Also, it is appropriate for you to ask what the next steps are in the review process such as another meeting, a decision, a reference check, etc. It is not appropriate, however, to ask about salary, vacation days, and any other perks. Only once an offer is extended is it appropriate to discuss these topics. Refer to pages 86 and 87 in the Appendix for a list of appropriate questions for you to ask.

One of the most important questions you will have to answer is, "Why should we hire you, take a chance on you, or invest our money in you?" Here is where you have to show that you are the best candidate and how you stand out from the others competing for the same opportunity. It is very important to know what they are looking for and what you have to offer and be able to back it up with examples and show that you are unique. As you can see, all of these questions require some preparation

Lori Bumgarner

and research on your part prior to walking in the door. To be better prepared for your upcoming interviews and meetings, work with a friend or interview and media coach on some role playing using the commonly asked interview questions found in the Appendix on pages 86.

Knowing the dos and don'ts

You must remember that, in addition to your responses and everything else you say, your every move is being watched, considered, and evaluated. Always keep the following dos and don'ts in mind:

- Do be on time. Showing up late indicates a lack of respect for the opportunity and for other people's time. Being on time is especially important in media interviews that are live on radio or television.
- As stated earlier, do be friendly to receptionists. Some executives observe how you treat their support staff. Also, many executives trust the opinions of their support staff and may ask them what they thought of you.
- Do follow the lead of the person meeting with you to identify relevant topics for conversation.
- Do bring extra copies of your information such as your resume, bio, press kit, CDs, etc.
- Do take notes and ask questions.
- Don't overstay your welcome or take up more time than was originally scheduled for the meeting.
- Don't chew gum or smoke.
- Don't ramble. Express your thoughts clearly and concisely.
- Don't be cocky or negative. Never badmouth a previous employer, colleague, or fellow artist in the industry.
- Don't watch the clock during your meeting.
- Don't bring up money until they do.

Following up

After your meeting or interview, it is a nice touch to follow up within 24 to 48 hours with a thank you note thanking everyone for taking the time to meet with you. Less than 10% of people actually do this, so if you are one of those 10%, you will be remembered for it. This is especially important if you have just finished a radio interview and you want to ensure the program director will put your song in rotation. In this particular case, go above and beyond what other artists do to show their appreciation.

Spend time going over any notes you may have taken during the interview, and review your responses to questions. Make note of how you responded, and always make sure to respond the same way to the same questions in any additional interviews so you are consistent in your answers. Use your notes to prepare for any second-round job interviews.

While awaiting a response following your job interview, continue your pursuit of other opportunities. Doing so will prevent you from wasting time and putting all your hope in one opportunity, and it may also give you some leverage when multiple offers start coming in. Also spend this time becoming familiar with money negotiation tactics and notifying your references that they may soon be contacted by the organizations. Always let your references know when you have accepted an offer, and take the time to thank them for their assistance.

Interviews can be very stressful and nerve-racking, but they don't have to be if you invest the time necessary to prepare for them and do your research. Doing so will allow you to exude the confidence you need to sell yourself!

Lori Bumgarner

Conclusion

"For attractive lips, speak words of kindness. For lovely eyes, seek out the good in people. For a slim figure, share your food with the hungry. For beautiful hair, let a child run his/her fingers through it once a day. For poise, walk with the knowledge that you never walk alone. People, even more than things, have to be restored, renewed, revived, reclaimed, and redeemed; never throw out anyone. Remember, if you ever need a helping hand, you will find one at the end of each of your arms. As you grow older, you will discover that you have two hands; one for helping yourself, and the other for helping others."
Audrey Hepburn

As you can see, building an image is a process. (Use the check list in the Appendix on page 95 to track your progress.) It takes time, patience, understanding, investment, an open mind, and a positive attitude to successfully build your image. Unfortunately, one small mistake can ruin an image in an instant. Lucky for us we have a God who forgives us and renews us, and friends who stand by us and encourage us. Image is something that runs deeper than one's appearance. We are all made in God's image, not just physically, but also spiritually. The Message Bible version of Colossians 3:12 states: "So, chosen by God for this new life of love, dress in the wardrobe God picked out for you: compassion, kindness, humility, quiet strength, discipline. Be even-tempered, content with second place, quick to forgive an offense. Forgive as quickly and completely as the Master forgave you. And regardless of what else you put on, wear love. It's your basic, all-purpose garment. Never be without it." This is a wardrobe that is one-size-fits-all and never goes out of style!

Appendix

Garment Review Form

```
┌─────────────────────────────┐
│                             │
│                             │
│                             │
│       Place photo of        │
│     garment/outfit here.    │
│                             │
│                             │
│                             │
│                             │
└─────────────────────────────┘
```

Garment/Outfit: _____

Store where purchased: _____

Price/Value of garment: _____

Date purchased: _____

Size: _____

Dates worn and event:

_____ _____

_____ _____

_____ _____

_____ _____

_____ _____

Items from closet this garment coordinates with:

_____

_____

_____

_____

When I wear this outfit I feel…

_____

_____

When I wear this outfit others say I look…

_____

_____

End of season evaluation of garment

Number of times worn during season: _____

Current fit of garment (i.e. too big, too small, etc.):

_____

Current condition of garment (i.e. good, fair, poor, etc.):

_____

Current style of garment (i.e. is it a classic still in style, is it a trend that is now outdated, does the style of the garment fit your current lifestyle?)

_____

_____

Next steps: (circle one)

Clean and store for next season | Alter/repair | Donate/consign | Toss

Shopping list of items needed to update this garment:

_____

_____

_____

Lori Bumgarner

Online Self-Audit

Is the email address on your resume or business card professional or cute/funny?

Professional | Cute/funny

If you circled "cute/funny," is that appropriate for what you do professionally?

Yes | No

How often do you Google yourself?

Regularly | Occasionally | Rarely | Never

When you do, are you comfortable with what you find?

Yes | No

For each of your social networking pages, would you feel comfortable if anyone other than your friends (i.e. potential employers) were to see your:

Profile?
Yes | No

Photos?
Yes | No

Tweets and Comments?
Yes | No

Friends' comments?
Yes | No

Friends' photos of you?
Yes | No

Groups or fan pages you belong to?
Yes | No

Do you have a resume, bio, or music posted on any career or music sites?

Yes | No

If yes, is your resume, bio, or music current?

Yes | No

Are you familiar with the site's privacy policies?

Yes | No

If you have your own web site or blog, would you be comfortable if a potential employer or industry leader were to read its contents?

Yes | No

Have you ever discussed a company or label, job, job interview, supervisor, employee, industry leader, etc. by name on your blog or web site?

Yes | No

Do you include anything on your blog or web site you wouldn't want your grandmother to see or you wouldn't want splashed on the front page of the newspaper?

Yes | No

Based on your answers to the questions above, are you comfortable with the image you are presenting online?

Yes | No

If you answered "no," what steps can you take to improve your online image?

_____

_____

Continued

Lori Bumgarner

Consider the areas that need the most work (i.e. social networking profiles, online resumes, music promotion pages, etc.).

What can you correct immediately?

_____

_____

What is going to take some time and research?

_____

_____

What might require ongoing maintenance?

_____

_____

Identify some goals and steps to improve your online image:
1. _____
2. _____
3. _____
4. _____
5. _____

Adapted from "Personal Internet Presence Jobseeker Self-Audit" form, *NACE Journal*, Summer 2006.

Resume Guidelines

- A resume is a marketing tool, not a complete job history. Include only the items that will help you get the job you want. Leave off anything that won't. Try to target your resume to a specific position or industry.
- Your resume should be one to two *full* pages in length, but preferably only one full page.
- Your document should look balanced, be pleasing to the eye, and be easy to read.
- Your resume format (bolding, italics, etc.) must be consistent throughout your document.
- The body text should not be too small (no less than 10 pt.) or too large (no more than 12 pt.).
- Use consistent and proper punctuation.
- The phone number you include in your contact information should go to a professional sounding outgoing voicemail message.
- Do not use personal pronouns like "me" and "I."
- Keep your objective short and concise by simply stating the industry and/or job title and the company name (for example, "Seeking position as account executive with XYZ Company").
- List all information in reverse chronological order.
- If you have been out of school for more than five years, list your education after your experience.
- Within the education section, list your degree first, then the name of the school.
- Within the experience section, list your job title first, then the name of the company.
- List job descriptions and duties with bullets instead of writing them in paragraph form, and use strong action words in the appropriate verb tense to describe what you did in your past jobs. (Avoid using passive phrases such as "responsible for" and "duties included.")

Continued

Lori Bumgarner

- Include figures in your past job descriptions to quantify what you accomplished.
- Do not include a list of professional references. This should be a separate document in the same format as your resume.
- It is unnecessary to include a statement at the bottom of your resume that refers to the availability of your references. However, you may want to include a statement at the bottom of your resume that lets the reader know that you have a professional portfolio for review or to share.
- Run a spell check AND proofread carefully. You should also get at least two additional people to proofread your resume.

Networking Goals

- Get quality business cards printed that include your name and contact information. Use a design that makes your card different from others, even if that means just including a professional photo of yourself on the card (but only if it is appropriate in your particular industry you are targeting to include a photo). In other words, don't end up using inexpensive business card templates that several other people may be using. You don't want your card to get lost in the shuffle by looking like everyone else's!

- Develop and perfect your elevator speech and make it flexible so that it can be responsive to the agenda and needs of the listener. Be prepared to expand on it with more information or to hold back and provide just a sound bite when appropriate. To put it all together, start by writing a brief summary of your resume or your bio. Next, write a description of what you are doing now and what your goals are for both the immediate and the long-term future. Also, consider a question you can tag onto the end of your elevator speech that could open a two-way discussion. It's always best to use a question that shows interest in what the listener may have to share about themselves. Finally, memorize your elevator speech to the point where you can say it easily and naturally.

- Schedule at least three informational interviews.

- Send thank you notes to informational interviewees within 24 hours of the interview.

- Schedule informational interviews with the people your previous interviewees referred you to.

- Attend at least _____ networking events each month or each quarter. (You set your own goal for the amount of events you want to attend.)

- Make at least _____ new connections at each event. (You set your own goal for the amount of new connections you plan to make at each event.)

- Follow up with each contact made within one to two weeks of event.

- Continue to foster the relationships you have made thus far while building new ones.

Lori Bumgarner

Commonly Asked Job Interview Questions

Common questions you may be asked:

- Can you tell me about yourself?
- What is your greatest strength?
- What is your greatest weakness?
- What are your long-range goals?
- What do you know about us?
- Can you tell me about a time when you've gone above and beyond what was expected of you?
- Can you tell me about a time when you had to deal with a difficult work situation or a difficult employee or co-worker? How did you handle the situation?
- What was the last book you read? (Yes, this is a question that comes up often in job interviews, and yes, they want to see that you're doing more than just any required reading you may have.)
- Why should we hire you?
- Do you have any questions for us?

Questions you should ask:

- What is a typical day like on this particular job or at this particular company?
- How do the people who work here like their jobs and the company?
- Are there opportunities for training and advancement?
- Why is this position open?
- Who will I be working with directly?
- What will be one of the first projects I will be involved in if hired?

- Do team members and co-workers typically eat lunch together, or do they typically eat lunch at their desks?
- What's the most important thing I can do to help this organization within the first 90 days of my employment?
- What are the next steps in the hiring process?
- Are there any issues or concerns about my candidacy that I can address at this time?

Note: also include questions you came up with during your research. Avoid questions pertaining to salary and vacation, holiday, or sick leave and other perks.

Lori Bumgarner

Guidelines for Meetings with Labels and Music Publishers

General guidelines:

- Expect that your meeting will last only about 20 minutes, 30 minutes if you're lucky.
- Be prepared to perform right then and there.
- Be prepared to perform your best or favorite song and your worst or least favorite song. (Have your guitar or a guitarist with you.)
- Look like a star! Dress the part and help them see they don't have to spend a lot of time and money on you to make you look better. They are looking for someone who is already the total package.
- Don't talk too much or too little. Don't give just one-word answers, but also don't ramble.
- Be yourself, but BE HUMBLE!
- If they are interested in you, they will probably have you come back for a couple more interviews. Don't let their continued interest make you cocky. STAY HUMBLE!
- Be consistent with the answers you gave to questions in previous meetings or interviews.

Common questions you may be asked:

- Who are you? Who is (your name or your band's name)? In other words, what is the meaning of you and your art? (Be specific.)
- What image do you think your music conveys?
- Define yourself or your band in one word or one sentence.
- What makes you unique and different from other acts?
- What's your story? (Everyone has a story. Be specific and descriptive about yours.)
- Do you write your own songs?
- What are your songs about?

- What are your best or favorite three songs of yours?
- What are your worst or least favorite three songs?
- Who are your musical influences?
- Who do you sound like, and whom do you compare yourself to?
- Who is your demographic?
- Do you have a business plan for your music career?
- What exactly are you marketing?
- How many live performances do you do in a year? (Here they are looking to see if you are seasoned or experienced.)
- Where do you see yourself in 5 years?
- What sacrifices are you willing to make to do what you want to do?
- Are you willing to let the record label own the publishing on your songs? (Here they are looking to see how serious you are.)
- Are you willing to change your look?
- What do you know about us?
- Why should we invest our money in you?
- Have you already signed any other deals with publishers, producers, etc.? (You must be honest and up front about this!)
- I don't think you're good enough. (Here they may be looking to see how you react to this statement and to see if you give up easily. Show that you have the ability to handle rejection in a healthy and appropriate manner.)

Questions you should ask the label:

- What kind of support is provided for new roster members at the label?
- What are the specific terms of your offer?
- Can I get back to you after I've had a chance to review your offer with my lawyer?

Continued

Lori Bumgarner

Questions you should ask yourself:

- Am I able to do everything the label is offering on my own without the help of a label?
- Am I willing to give over the control of my career to a label?
- What are my deal breakers?
- Where can I find a good attorney who specializes in entertainment law that can review with me the offer from the label?

Guidelines for Media Interviews

General Tips:

- Read, listen to, and watch others' media interviews with a critical eye. Learn from their strengths and their weaknesses.
- Do your research. Know the stats about the magazine, radio station, or TV show and know the demographics of their audience such as its median age.
- Be yourself instead of trying to look or sound like what you think you're supposed to look and sound like, but always try to be your best you (more polished, prepared, on your best behavior, and looking your best).
- Always listen to the question and how it is asked, and answer it the way it is asked. For example, if you are asked a two-part question, always answer both parts. It's okay to ask the interviewer to repeat the 2nd part of the question if you've forgotten what it is.
- Don't be a chatter box, but also don't be timid or give one-word answers. Provide sound bites.
- Always provide interesting stories and funny anecdotes that paint a picture for the listener or viewer and support the point you are making.
- Never be defensive or combative with the interviewer.
- Don't forget to give a plug for your latest show, event, project, book, or CD. Let the audience know where they can get these and more information by giving your web site.

Radio:

- Refine your diction. Commit to record yourself during actual conversations so you'll recognize your weak spots, and start correcting them. Repetitive speech mannerisms become much more distracting when heard on the radio and over the phone.

Continued

Lori Bumgarner

- Use your interviewer's first name when responding to his or her questions. If doing a phone interview, use the DJ's name more often than you would in a face-to-face interview.

- Treat it like a regular conversation. You wouldn't have a normal conversation with someone where you only talk about yourself. DJ's have big egos, so ask them about what's been going on with them. Mention how you heard about one of the station's most recent events. (This is where your research comes in.) Tell the DJ how much you appreciate his or her listeners. For every 2-3 things you say about yourself, say something good about the DJ or the station, but make sure it's genuine.

- Use positive body language even though you won't be seen by your listener (i.e. smile, use gestures and facial expressions, etc.). Positive body language impacts all of the vocal nuances of speech.

- Match your speaking pace with the DJ's speaking pace. Don't speak too fast or too slow.

- Match your volume level with the DJ's volume level.

- For phoners, always try to be on a land line if possible, and disable your call waiting.

- If doing the interview in the radio station's studio, still dress appropriately. They may be streaming live video from their studio on their web site.

Television:

- Open yourself out to the camera somewhat. Don't be too engaged (squarely faced) with the person interviewing you.

- Wear mid-tone colors. (Good colors for TV are mid-tone blues and violets.) Avoid colors that are extremely too light (white, oatmeal), too dark (black, especially if your back drop is black), or too bright. Avoid wearing red if possible because it can sometimes create a fuzzy halo effect on camera.

- Wear solids instead of bold prints or small prints. Small prints (thin stripes especially) can cause that dizzy flashing effect on screen.

- Don't wear jewelry that makes a lot of noise when you move (i.e. clanky bracelets).
- Don't wear anything that will reflect the bright lights (i.e. smooth or shiny jewelry).

Print:

- Print interviews are a lot more laid back and relaxed than radio and TV interviews.
- Print interviews last longer and are more in-depth. In these interviews you must provide more information than you would in a quick television or radio interview so the writer can develop an in-depth story.
- You should provide "quotable quotes." Again, paint a picture of your story with your words.

Commonly asked questions:

- In radio and TV interviews, you will be asked about your latest projects, your upcoming shows, and the latest news that is out about you.
- In print interviews, you will be asked about your background, what you were like growing up, and how you became an artist.
- In radio interviews you may have to field questions from fans calling into the station which can be pretty much about anything!
- In all interviews you are likely to be asked who your influences are and how you go about writing or choosing your songs.

Lori Bumgarner

Advance Your Image

Tracking Your Progress

As stated earlier, building your image is a process that takes time, patience, effort, and commitment. Below is a list of the steps discussed in the previous chapters to help you track your progress. There are even smaller steps within each of these steps you must take to accomplish each one. This checklist and the advice listed in the previous chapters are designed to help you break the process down into more manageable steps.

- ☐ Review current wardrobe.
- ☐ Shop for items needed to supplement current wardrobe.
- ☐ Get clothing tailored.
- ☐ Update hairstyle and/or eyeglass frames.
- ☐ Draft, proofread, and update bio, resume, and cover letter.
- ☐ Review and clean up online presence.
- ☐ Create elevator speech.
- ☐ Research the industry and its key players.
- ☐ Conduct informational interviews.
- ☐ Implement networking strategies.
- ☐ Research the industry's companies and organizations.
- ☐ Determine appropriate attire for meetings and interviews.
- ☐ Prepare for commonly asked job and/or media interview questions.
- ☐ Prepare questions to ask in the job interview or label meeting.
- ☐ Send a thank you note immediately following your meetings and interviews.

Lori Bumgarner

Notes

_____
_____
_____
_____
_____
_____
_____
_____
_____
_____
_____
_____
_____
_____
_____
_____
_____
_____
_____
_____
_____
_____
_____
_____
_____
_____
_____
_____
_____
_____
_____
_____

Notes

_____
_____
_____
_____
_____
_____
_____
_____
_____
_____
_____
_____
_____
_____
_____
_____
_____
_____
_____
_____
_____
_____
_____
_____
_____
_____
_____
_____
_____
_____
_____
_____
_____
_____

Lori Bumgarner

Notes

_____

_____

_____

_____

_____

_____

_____

_____

_____

_____

_____

_____

_____

_____

_____

_____

_____

_____

_____

_____

_____

_____

_____

_____

_____

_____

_____

_____

_____

_____

_____

_____

_____

Advance Your Image

Notes

_____

About the Author

Image consultant, speaker, and author Lori Bumgarner assists recording artists, music industry professionals, and other professionals in developing an image and personal brand to advance their careers. As the owner of paNASH Style LLC, a Nashville-based image consulting company that provides wardrobe styling and interview coaching services, Lori has worked with a variety of clients including award-winning artists, video chart toppers, music industry executives, professional athletes and entertainers, entrepreneurs, recent college graduates, and more.

Lori's advice has been featured in The Wall Street Journal's online blog, WSMV-TV's Better Nashville, and WVOL radio where Oprah Winfrey began her broadcasting career, and she has written for various magazines and newspapers on topics such as networking and dressing for success. Her speaking engagements have included presentations for the Nashville Songwriters Association International (NSAI) and the O'More College of Design Image Conservatory.

Lori possesses a combined 15 years experience in career coaching (most recently at Vanderbilt University), media coaching, and image consulting. She holds a master of education degree from the University of South Carolina and a bachelor of arts degree in psychology from the University of North Carolina at Charlotte, and most recently received additional styling training in New York City directly under the tutelage of Stacy London (TLC's *What Not To Wear*).

For more information on Lori's services,
visit her web site at www.paNASHstyle.com.

Readers interested in scheduling an initial consultation with Lori or booking
her for a speaking engagement can contact her at LoriB@paNASHstyle.com.

CPSIA information can be obtained at www.ICGtesting.com
Printed in the USA
LVOW06s1353100715

445774LV00001B/172/P